# BIBLE REFLECTIONS

## Journeys of the mind

## DR. RODERICK LONEY

LITTLE ARK MEDIA
PRINCETON

BIBLE REFLECTIONS
Journeys of the Mind

info@littlearkmedia.com
www.LittleArkMedia.com


ISBN: 978-0615618043

Cover & Interior by Rock Spaceship Media

# CONTENTS

# INTRODUCTION

There is beauty and a rhythm in the language of the scriptures that is often overlooked in the pursuit of meaning. This collection of Bible principles is congruent with God's meaning but attempts to catch a vision of that beauty. It is hoped that the format of this presentation might make it easier for some to understand the message of the Bible.

Above all, those who hear the Word of God need to be reminded constantly that God's meaning is inaccessible to those who by human wisdom seek to understand His Word. God uses the language of men figuratively in order to communicate the mysteries of His Will. Its terms are only revealed as one compares scripture with scripture (1 Cor.1:21; 2:13; Isa.28:13).

My hope is that the meaning of man's life as revealed in God's Truth may be seen in a clearer perspective as it is presented *in verse.*

CHAPTER ONE

# EVERY MAN'S DREAMS

### 1. WANNA BE

Time sets the frame-of-reference
For all we are, will be
For what we see, and hear, and think
Have power; They-Shape-"Me"
Our knowledge, dreams, or fantasies are rooted in the soul
But all of life's activities are fleeting, growing old
There is no other boundary that measures life for us
The range of time on earth is sealed
Choose God or become dust

"Was" passes on, and "will" may never be
All man's life but a moment of sorrow, even for *me*
To be or not to be is but, a summary of time
It sets the path for all things made, the plan of God sublime
Both man and beast and creeping thing
All plants and insects, birds on wing
Each life is but a span of time
One heartbeat, one swallow, one breath of air, one spark
One moment to be *mine*

But God created many things
Each for its time and season
Bits, moments, stitched together, each with its rhyme and
reason
For some its brief for others long, but all part of a plan
That God has set in motion to rescue fallen man
Thus who I be, what God will see
Not memories, or dreams, or hopes to be
My Faith should be the summary, of time allotted me
It only is the path that measures me, if I must BE

The life of man more than the span
Of years he lives on earth
Or even that of knowing how long he'll be from birth
He may be up, or may be down, a fool at times or but a clown
But not his dreams nor deeds unbound,
Or things he owns, or prestige found
Will measure time by which he's bound
His life on earth is but one round,
Only by faith **I'LL BE**, when Christ is found in me

**"He that heareth my word...
is passed from death unto Life" (John 5:24).**

## 2. I BE
I cannot ask the question
"To be or not to be"
For God already answered
When HE created Me

I "was" before I came "to be"
Conceived enshrined a zygote free
In utero to grow unseen
Like fish, or frog, a water-being

Then suddenly a door was open
The water-being was now a token
Of life as free from lines constraining
A social creature, caterwauling

The "WAS" had now become an "IS"
Named, and slotted ready to live
To move along the paths of men
To search and find the "If" and "When"

Ready to hear the question then
Not just "to be" but "to begin"
A path of life that's freed from sin
If Jesus Savior entered in.

No longer let the question be
"To be" I say "or Not to be"
For if in Christ I become "Me"
Then alas "I be"

Freed from the old
Nurtured in sin
Saved by God's Grace
At peace within, I-I-I-Beeee
**"If the Son therefore shall make you free,
ye shall be free indeed" (John 8:36)**

4

# 3. YOUR NAME, BOY

Little boy, little boy what's your name?
"Pee-a-bed, pee-a-bed" cry for shame
And that was the name for some little boys
Who wetted their beds, no joys, no toys

For life most times was very sad
There was so little to make one glad
'Twas fights and groans of discontent
For food was lacking and money for rent

So Jim and Johnny now three and four
Must understand that dad is poor
And mammy can't work she has no skills
And life is made up of paying bills

I've seen these children eyes open wide
Face pressed on glass looking inside
Through the store window I see the tears
Etched on young faces the burden of years

But even for children disabled by need
The Light of the Gospel can change them indeed
Though poor and dejected and wetting their bed
God's Word will transform them to God's Seed instead

When Jesus comes in the hopeless have hope
The children neglected will learn how to cope
No longer to sleep disturbed and bed wet
God brings them new life a name for them yet

**"Neither is there salvation in any other name...
whereby we must be saved" (Acts 4:12)**

5

## 4. GLOSS OR GLORY (cf. 1 Sam.15:9)

Though I should live to be
The longest-living person one would see
And though my hoary head
Moves right along as living with the dead
Yet all the time I'll ever have is NOW
Though all the world itself before me bow

Should all the world seem awestruck at the "fire"
Which blazed a life-trail so as to aspire
And from a life that promised but so little
There could arise this tower of strength and mettle
Yet all that I could ever yet become
Will be a fleeting moment in God's sun

What I be could ne'er be etched in stone
No mortal man becomes it to his bone
What opportunity or talent brings his way
When men ascribe great honors to his day
Yet all his time on earth who he will be
Will keep on changing like waves of the sea

No man could ever really hope to BE
Much longer than the crossing of a "T"
What is achieved by heart or hands or head
Is after-glow of light which had him led
Yet deep inside the basic maps that be
Are footprints on the way becoming me

It may be that a man might well achieve
High status, lofty rank and feel the "breeze"
As new-found power filters through his hand
Thinks to himself "surely I must be grand"
Yet all the time it's wise for him to see
He's lost who loses sight of "basic ME"

And when the power and prestige of his day
Evaporates and leaves him on the way
He will be lost if nothing he can find
To bind and heal the sickness of his mind
Yet all conditions had he in control
But then he strayed and gave away his soul

So if today you find yourself a-basking
Within the grip of power "everlasting"
Take heed less you too lose your grip
Upon that self, that **you,** that holds the ship
Yet as it happens oft so many a time
Man is confused for "Gloss" looks like "Sublime"

**"...now is the accepted time;
behold, now is the day of salvation" (2 Cor.6:2)**

## 5. FINDING ME

"I am" will always be my fate
E'en when I stand at heaven's gate
No more, or less of me can be
The image of God has bounded me

My past is always history
My future yet to be
My life a state of mystery
Wondering to be, or not to be

Man speaks of what he sees in me
God knows the all of what I'll be
At times these things are quite confusing
"I am", "I be", is lost in musing

I ponder on what was that me
That men have seen or that I sought to be
I even wonder out aloud
How God would set me on a cloud

I think of heaven as my home
Out of the reach of men unknown
To walk the streets of gold up there
I think of "am" as me in air

But no, a dream this has to be
That God indeed will transform me
Cause me to fly on angel's wings
Make me to rise to heavenly things?

Awake to faith heaven's not a dream
God's grace can change the vile to clean
He's sent His Son to ransom me
And now all His forever I'll be

"Unclean" "unclean" no more to be
For living water entered me
My soul's transformed the "am" the "me" the what will be
Now part of God's Eternity, "I'm free"

**"Those things, which ye have both learned and received, and heard, and seen in me, do: and the God of Peace shall be with you" (Phil.4:9)**

# CHAPTER TWO

# MIRRORS ANYONE

## 6. HIDDEN TRAILS

I stumbled in the darkness
That stone was hidden from me
Yet all along 't was in my path
Right there for all to see

But now that I had stumbled
I stopped to take a look
With flashing light and keen insight
I sought it by the book

It soon became apparent
The stone that caused my fall
Was not upon the ground ahead
But hid within my walls

Deep set within my memory
Past images came to light
Of scenes now etched within my soul
That caused my failing sight

For deep within the mind of man
Experiences lie hidden
These oft may cause a stumble
When past and present "rumble"

The things I've heard and seen and done
Have framed the me I am
My home, my school, my models
Foundations of life's plan

They set the pace, make life a race
T'ween yesterdays and now
The hurts, rejections, sobs and pains
Leave traces that constrain my veins, I bow

These form the hidden trail
That cause my steps to fail
When "past" will yet prevail
Push "present" off the rail, life in travail

**"But have renounced the hidden things of dishonesty...
commending ourselves to every man's conscience in the sight
of God" (2 Cor.4:2)**

# 7. AND SO, BATHSHEBA

A man named David
Looked and saw
A woman bathing on the floor
He just could not believe his eyes
For what he saw did tantalize
He sent a messenger to find
Where she did live, and would she mind
If he could call on her sometime
Or she would visit that'd be fine
For he and she might work out well
As long as none their tale would tell
And so before you say "Jack Sprat"
Bathsheba lay on David's mat
A trysting time they had as well
Things worked out so, no one would tell
But on one somber day much later
News came to David from one quite Greater
Who all along was looking in
And saw the King fall into sin
"No, no" said David can this be
This dear woman no longer free
To visit with me now and then
Must trysting time come to an end?
Indeed it must
The secret trust is now a bust
The woman is quite pregnant thus
Now all the world will rise and be
In judgment on the King so he
An end to these things he must bring
He surely needs "friend of the king"
For there must be a way to bend
Those things that are not in the trend

The husband of this woman fair
Must bear the blame and clear the air
The husband dutifully came
A man, a soldier, Uriah his name
But he, repeatedly would not
Bed down his wife while war was hot
So ultimately it was planned
He should see danger under-manned
And thus in battle he would die
So David could conceal his lie
And so things seemed to work out well
But "Nat" the prophet rang the bell
When Nathan said unto the King
"Thou art the man" to thee I bring
The tidings of thy God and King
In heart and mind and spirit bent
David the King was penitent
He cried to God that mercy He
Might grant the king thou vile he be
And thus the man from sin did pass
All was Forgiven, Free at last.

**The Lord...is not willing that any should perish,
but that all should come to repentance (2 Pet.3:9)**

## 8. THE EQUALIZER (cf. Heb.9:27)

Here in your privacy you sit alone
No one to share your space, King on your throne
Royalty sits here too, 'tis common ground
This is that venue where all men must sit down

Each hears a common call none turns away
All respond quickly strive to obey
Even recalcitrants spring to alert
None dare resist the urge this is no time to flirt

High and low rich and poor come to this seat
Take their position, here, all are meek
Wait for instructions not in control
Bear every burden, no disdain, frown, or curl

Some respond quickly anxious to please
Happy to answer finding an ease
Others may "phart" even grunt or groan
But glad to surrender with simply a moan

Isn't it funny, this common ground
All men must share it, no special one is found
What so we put in, take through the mouth
Will head for the exit soon to come out

So, all men are really equal, each one, servant to sin.
Tuned to a non-stop timer ticking inside, within
In due course comes the call, "time's up", we must depart
Heaven for the chosen, Hell only for the "smart"

Just like the natural call that no one can ignore
So too the heavenly voice is knocking at your door
Should you dare to ignore it there is a price to pay
Not simple humiliation but Hell, and that's the way

Come now says the Savior let's reason today
Even sins that are scarlet will all be washed away
Nature will soon be calling, you'll visit here again
But at earth's final call, it's the end of your reign

So face it now friend, even that stubborn you
Must rise to obey nature's call when nothing else will do
Is heaven's call less urgent, nothing but sublime
Does nature's call mean more to you than that which ends your time?

**"And hath made of one blood all nations of men...
on all the face of the earth" (Acts 17:26)**

### 9. UNFINISHED DREAM - WILLIE (cf. Prov.20:1)

How sweetly do the voices sing
As Heralds, Angels, come to bring to me, an Offering
Visions of life, scenes of the sea
Glimpses of friends long-departed from me
Through winding tunnels did I glide and lighted exits on the
side
So full of fear and prone to hide
Until at last, at length, LIGHTS, the other side
To pastures green through which I wander
Confused, puzzled so much to ponder
Considering all that this might be
Familiar faces and all this company to welcome me
Old barroom buddies too, so long unseen
To bring me to the silver lake that lies between
And here and there the waterspouts like sentinels are standing
Denying access to the other side, the point of landing
I see it vaguely now as in a mist
Shadows and outlines of that place of Heavenly Bliss
Here I must wait, the boat will soon come sailing
To ferry me across this moat to pleasures never failing
Then, suddenly, alas, I hear the bells a-pealing
The sounds of trumpets beckon, my mind reeling

***So, listen Well,*** <u>the</u> <u>voice</u> <u>alone</u> can tell
Whether your journey takes you, to **Heaven** or into
***H - e - e - e - ll***
To live or die is now the cry
The trumpet sounds do cease
Everything here changes, I Enter the garden of peace

But then come other voices
Softly, too gentle e'en to hear
But Soon they become thunderclaps breaking upon my ear
The scene has changed "*oh horrors <u>No</u>, there is no pleasure here,*
I see the flames - I hear the fire - filling my soul with fear
**With God,** in heaven I am not, the pleasant scenes were only "Butts"
The rest were <u>Sparkles in the Cup</u>
Libation is out – M Y  T I M E  I S  U P"
Deception packages were they, to keep me from the "Narrow" way
For by my senses I was led, they made for me all Hell as bed
I thought my soul was bound for heaven, my fantasies were really leaven
Thank God this was but all A DREAM my life is not just all a scene
Here I am no spectator, an actor I am not,
My life is in the Hand of God, no "Ifs" or "Ands" or "cigar butts"
God grant the grace, give me the space, let me become, and be
At peace within my soul, all heaven-bound and free
Give me the Faith that turns my life from <u>nip</u> and <u>tip</u> to Thee
Help me to know the Second Birth, give me the grace to SEE
Transform my life while here on Earth, I linger
Let me no longer to my lip lift finger to hold a "Butt" or kiss deceptive Cup

**"There is a way which seemeth right ..., but the end thereof are the ways of death" (Prov.14:12)**

# CHAPTER THREE

# EVERY WIFE AN "EVE"

### 10. OF ONE FLESH

The man is sitting all alone, bored, much but unafraid
Hoping that the Father would, come quickly to his aid
By naming animals he knew that he was all alone
And he would need Help-Meet complete one, of his very bone

In due course God had heard him, a woman for the man
That was the very basis of Father's Divine plan
To bind them both together make of Two, only One
Blending their Resources to bring to birth a Son

No Loose Arrangement was God's Plan
For that would just Weaken and Desecrate man
It might seem a Haven for Sexual bliss
But surely will leave all Offspring Amiss

Rootless and trackless they'll not have a nest
A place to find comfort, a base to find Rest
For each child a Nook or Cranny'll be home
A Berth, a Hang-out, a new stepping stone

Loose Sex has its hazards for women and men
A base of frustrations all "now," nothing "then"
Parading as love but only a farce
Concealing all truth by wearing a Mask

God's Plan is the greatest come weal or come woe
When all is considered it just will be so
No way will be found to offer a plan
More suited to meet every issue of man

Adultery beckons but that way marks Debt
And all Fornication is part of the set
One-Fleshed in the spirit is God's only Plan
For lasting relations between "Wo" and "man"

**"Therefore shall a man leave his father and his mother, and
shall cleave unto his wife: and they shall be one flesh"
(Gen.2:24)**

## 11. DREAMING IN PARADISE

So God had come where Adam was lying
Brooding in silence, alone, but not crying
'Tis not that the man was enduring distress
He was living in Eden, completely at rest

Yet deep in his heart the man did discern
The need for companion, woman all his own
Like all the created life round about
He too needed company of that 'twas no doubt

Someone like himself with whom he could share
All of God's blessings so very very near
A Help-Meet who always at his side would stand
Together fulfilling God's stated demands

Without her, alone, none could multiply
Not replenish the earth however hard he might try
Thus God in His wisdom designed a full plan
To fulfill His purpose for making woman

**"And the LORD God planted a garden eastward in Eden; and there he put the man whom he had formed" (Gen.2:8)**

## 12. TWO FACES OF EVE

So God had come to know for sure
That Adam needed more much more
Than animals to name and tame
Or birds to play the garden game
Man had a duty to fulfill
If he should strive to do God's will
Alone he could not fill the earth
With sons and daughters or give birth
Therefore for man God had to make
Someone to give what it would take

Out of the body of the man
God planned, designed, fashioned wo-man
Her name was Eve all-tuned to please
Programmed to put the man at ease
What Adam saw just could not be
"That God would make a wife for me"
Help-Meet she was and sorely needed
God had replied when Adam pleaded
But ere she reached a helping hand
The Help-Meet stumbled, she had her plan

Not Adam to please or God obey
She consorted with Satan she'd have it her way
Thus in the beginning, the woman sinned
She turned to her husband and he too, she pinned
The serpent was happy, dominion he had
Old Satan was gloating while Adam was sad
And thus it began the tale of a man
Pathway of Woe, Disobedience, "bigam"?
So God intervened a Promise He made
To vanquish the power that sought to invade
To turn Death to Life the slave to be free
God fashioned a plan to sanctify me
As Eve was the agent to introduce sin
So, God would now use her to bring Jesus in

**"...Be Fruitful, and multiply, and replenish the earth, and subdue it"**
**(Gen.1:28)**

## 13. FOOTPRINTS OF EVE

The earth a silent mass, brooding in darkness
The stillness echoing the sound, "Let there be Light"
And then from everywhere there came, Shards of Brightness
Light kissing darkness, heaven all aflame

Six days have passed, a period wrapped in wonder
Life starts to be, creeping, running, flying, everywhere a tree
And then another voice is heard, the garden-keeper, not a bird
Man has come forth, made in God's image, by His Word

Out of the body of the man God had Himself carved out a plan
Help-Meet to be, One-fleshed, bonded, Free
And then THE God pronounced them "Good"
They knew the tree, and what Obedience should

To Eve, God had not said a Word of covering the head
Her hair hung low beneath her waist so nothing need be said
She knew full well the differences that God had put in place
To mark her as a woman, and mother of the race

But then, despite these differences
She did confuse her role
She ran ahead of Adam, a Help-Meet making Bold
Forsaking her assignment, Usurping we are told
So by that act, it is a fact
That Eve being out of turn, all men will surely burn

Thus from that day in every way
New rules were put in place
To help all of Eve's daughters to win God's Divine Race
"A Hat for Eve," God said it
She needs a double sign
To reckon with the angels, and keep God's Word in mind

Her hair, a natural covering
The Hat, a Veil Divine
What more could be required
True beauty shining out of Ashes, God in mind
Eve must no longer set aside the will of God and man
God help her to surrender, lift high Salvation's Plan

**"For this cause ought the woman to have power on her head
Because of the angels" (1 Cor.11:10)**

## 14. ADAM AND EVE, REFLECTIONS

Not once, but many times, or often
Adam may to Eve have spoken
Of the tree that God had said
If you eat, you will be dead

"How could that be?" Eve may have thought
"Could such a fruit be good for naught?
Could it thus hide beneath its bark
The kiss of death the final mark?"

It made no sense to Eve at least
That such a fruit could be a *beast*
Hiding beneath its sweet perfume
The kiss of death pathway to doom

Was Eve a-sulking on the side
Thinking, the thoughts she tried to hide?
If so, the wily Serpent thought
She may be easy to be *bought*

Asking her about the tree
And God's command of what should be
Serpent talk quite soon revealed
How much mere power she could wield

How wonderful and wise she thought
Could it be just my "good" he sought
The words he spoke sounded so sure
Would she indeed know *So Much More?*

Irreligious though the thought
Deceived she was and all for naught
Should she now let her Adam know
God really had not said it so?

Perhaps just what the serpent said
Could place them so much more ahead
But could she from her husband hide
Just what she wanted to decide?

She made her choice she ate the fruit
Then came to Adam *looking cute*
She told him too in gentle words
That he should eat not only birds

So Adam thought Eve he *MUST* please
He could not leave her, like a breeze
So he decided he would take
Of that same fruit, not her forsake!

And then he looked, how could it be
"Is Eve all naked, did I see?"
And she to him then did reply
"Dear Adam, *Will I surely Die?*"

"That must not be," he thought, but then,
Slick serpent slipped into his den
Nowhere they found him though they looked
He fled the scene by hook and crook

Adam did cry, and Eve lament,
That God's clear Word they both had bent
"Let's hide from God" this was the thought
Perhaps a way out could be sought

So with the fig leaves they were covered
Filled with shame and things that bothered
Then behind the bushes they
Concealed themselves in every way

Filled with terror, how much they trembled
All around them the ground had rumbled
God was carrying out His rounds
As He went strolling through the grounds

25

When He drew near, they knew for certain
That soon He would be at their curtain
Bushes could not hide from Him
All the noise and all that din

Everywhere in Eden fair
Noise and noise now filled the air
All of nature in alarm
Exposed to death no longer calm

Suddenly, there was the Word
God was calling, and Adam heard
For God had said "where are you hiding
Are you no more in me abiding?"

Adam cried out "not *Me* Lord *She*
Of the fruit Eve gave to me"
And in my weakness I gave way
Fearing to lose her for "a day"

Eve also spoke chiming right in
How Slick the serpent made her sin
And how in fact she turned away
Hoping for a better day

Then God Himself looked all around
And found old "Slick" inside the ground
To him He said "dust shalt thou eat"
Slide on thy belly as is fitting and meet

But here the story does not end
For God had surely lost His friend
Consigned to death was he and she
No longer in God's company

And soon in time they saw no gain
In introducing sin and shame
Out of the Garden they must go
To face a world of weal and woe

The destiny of man to be
To Hell for all eternity
But then, the blessed Savior came
To cover Sin and take the Blame

**"...God hath said, Ye shall not eat of it...
I heard thy voice...and I was afraid, because I was naked"
(Gen.3:3-10)**

## 15. EVE UNBOUND

Not long it took the world to see
That Eve had left a legacy
A path to tread, a role to play
For every woman of today
Though one-fleshed she, "Help-Meet" to be
Resisted all authority
Would turn the rules both up and down
Around them all a way be found
That Eve might do her own desire
Come death or even come Hell fire
Her mind was bent on being free
From what she saw as not to be
Before no man would she yet bow
Despite her promise, pledge, or vow
She thought within herself that she
Would have the fruit "Pure Ecstasy"
She stretched her hand took of the tree
Ate of the fruit that should not be
And then to Adam quickly turned
Fearful, unsure, the morsel burned
"Help me" she says "turn not away
Come walk with me please let us stray"
He shuddered briefly at the thought
And then seduced no longer fought
Thus was it then the man was bought

But God has found a way to be
Where man has power over ecstasy
Transvestites are off their game
Men and women are not the same
But now with daughters everywhere
Too many Eves tempt man to share
Though Abraham had an Alternate
And David took Bathsheba's gate
The plan of God will man fulfill
When he's one fleshed in the Divine will
Spirit of God at work in the world
All men who are broken can now be made whole
Adam too Unbound, first thought that he was Free
And now for every Eve a brand new Destiny

**"The woman saw that the tree was good for food, and that it was pleasant to the eyes,... and did eat, and gave also unto her husband with her; and he did eat" (Gen.3:6)**

## 16. YES EVE

No truer words were ever spoken
Than that which Adam gave as token
For unto Eve he made quite clear
That none should come between them there

Not father, mother, friend or foe
For God had joined them weal or woe
And now one-fleshed they had become
Joined in the spirit two in one

But serpent did not heed the plan
Seduced the woman enticed the man
And now between the bonded pair
There was a difference that's not fair

Eve chose her way and Adam pondered
What should he do she surely blundered
Yet 'twas not long for him to think
She gave him fruit, "brought to the brink"

For out of man the woman came
He had to share, help take the blame
So of the fruit he also ate
And now they both were at the gate

Fallen they were both Adam and Eve
Naked, fearful, their home they must leave
Now God then gave them a brand new plan
New paths for survival not food on demand

From that day to this the tables have turned
Both Adam and Eve new lessons have learned
To stick to their vow to God they must bow
For He is the Shepherd for then and for now

And so to his Help-Meet Adam now said
That she must conform, by her man be led
And so as a binder to add to their pact
The given name "Eve" made all that a fact

**"And Adam called his wife's name Eve; because she was the mother of all living" (Gen.3:20)**

# CHAPTER FOUR

# BANISHED BUT REDEEMED

## 17. LIGHT OUT OF DARKNESS

The skies are now darkened, the clouds hide the sun.
Laboring on slowly as a day that is done
Its light too is tempered its glow a fading dawn.
As time itself is stumbling forgetting it is morn
The earth itself also, seems lifeless and dead
Because the man has sinned now darkness rules instead
I see him tottering on, as if about to fall, driven out of Eden,
    once and for all
Forlorn  he is, an outcast, rejected now by all
Pushed on by unseen  hands as those that caused the Fall
No hope within no help without His hiding place a leaf
And all of life seems, burdened by unbelief
No man can from himself escape, for all there is no hiding
But all along though hidden the love of God is biding.
The Grace of God is ever near reaching for a Berth
Trusting to hear somewhere within the distress of man's hurt
So now instead a sin-sick soul was struggling on the Earth
Then suddenly a voice was heard not of a beast or of a bird
The call again fell on his ear "Dear Adam tis me, I am here"
Turn to the light my hand you'd see
I am thy God who calleth thee bring all you burdens now to me
Forgiven I will set you free, **you still can be**
Look to the light my voice you'll hear
Know that your God is ever near
God's Word it says "come unto me all ye that labor" set you free
I am the God that healeth thee
But these reflections came to be when from Gods Word the man
    did flee

For  thoughts had formed within the woman who to the serpent
    went

How she could move to higher ground though she had not been
   sent
She turned her ears away from God as any fickle bird
Alas then sin's reality now plainly showed she erred
Nowhere it seems a place for dreams or hopes of turning back
Nowhere be free again, to stumble on God's track

There was no freedom to create for man an alternate
No place where weary spirits and souls in turmoil could
   hibernate
How could it be that that which offered thee the full of pleasure
Be so transformed in me that every lingering echo become a
   new measure
An arrow piercing to the heart and laying bare the bone
A servant of his own impulses man must be guided home

The man's name was Adam his wife was named Eve
Searching in vain for paths together through all the tangled
   weed
Hoping to find traces where even man could wander
Only one thing was constant the muffled sounds of thunder
As though the ground beneath their feet breathed fire, no relief.
A desert place, barren as far as eye could see
Separated from the God they loved, banished, no longer free
Doomed to wander where thorns and thistles bloom
And life arrayed in hostile garb comes to an end too soon

There might well be for every man some chance for a reprieve
In judgment God had promised it to those who would believe
For man although now fallen to live another day
God had in fact designed a pact to earn by toil and labor
Some of man's lot that was the plot of Eden when in favor
But now alas before these things themselves would come to pass
Adjustments must be made, no fork, no shovel, not even a s
How could it be that man once free was hindered on his journey
All that he took from Eden fair were coats of skin, no pony

No place to hide, no animal to ride, no tool to till the ground
For here he was not heaven-bound nor hoping to be found
At last the man began to reckon that all alone he was

33

E'en though his very company was sensitive, abuzz
He could not backwards turn the clock, nor reinvent the time
But surely now he sensed within, a spark of life sublime
As he sat for many days before the feet of God
The many things he learned from Him, a message from the Lord
Through thick and thin it served to strengthen him
So onward still he plodded, before a fountain stood
Water gushing, and all around the noise of living, good
Birds, insects, all beasts of the field joined in the refreshing
For even in this wilderness was evidence of blessing

Not far from where the waters flowed he saw amidst the rocks
A cavern which had fashioned out a place for taking stock
But as he drew much nearer his former friends had fled
Hastening quickly from him as though in fear and dread
In shock, dismayed, crestfallen, he did not understand
Until again it dawned on him that in the midst of all the din
The downs alone that sin had brought now changed the man
      within
Praise God for a new start the cave would be their home
Both he and Eve would do their best to answer that Divine
      request
To multiply, replenish, fill their nest **aloone...**

No wanderer he meant to be
But rather like a planted watered tree-to thrive
Adam knew Eve, she did conceive
From God she knew she would receive
She bore a son and called him Cain
And soon she did conceive again
Both sons were taught the fear of God
And learned the paths their parents trod
So on one day they both came near
Sounds of rejoicing filled the air
And hands weighed down with offering, made sacrifice

"Dear Lord and King to thee we bring the essence of our labor"
But ere they ventured out abroad the voice was clear, no favor

God spoke to them of many things, of deeds and ways and
    offering
Saying it often thus and so and how these things they ought to
    know
To Abel God had said quite clear "acceptable my son no fear"
But unto Cain rejection came he made a play, at his own game
Turning away from God's design to do that which was in his
    mind
Yet now he had God's disapproval, angry he was but yet quite
    frugal
In heart he turned away from God now bent on being his own
    lord
For Cain was in rebellion, rejecting God and brief
So thus it was an angry Cain went searching for relief

He found his brother Abel hoping to share his pain
But still he was quite angry his loss seemed Abel's gain
So as it was words were exchanged and Cain was mad again
He grabbed a nearby vessel and struck so there was pain
"Oh Abel brother Abel" by me your blood was shed
A vagabond I now will be and to my parents dead

And soon enough the truth was out
What Cain had done left none in doubt
The die was cast, no seed to be, finding grace in God's company
The death of Abel brought an end, so God no longer had a friend
Born of the woman, from Adam and Eve
Focused on God's will, Him only to please
Henceforth, the seed of Cain was only bent on gain
A different nation, born to evil, man in pain
Not seeking to be reconciled at all be understood
Much violence soon filled the earth for evil became

But then God raised another seed, Seth his name in word and
    deed
The God of heaven had blessed again, for Adam and Eve, no
    pain no pain
She did conceive, and bore a son by him God's work, will now be
    done

Through him God raised a man, named Noah, he preached, the
    Word of God is power

In time the heavens began to rain God's judgment on, the sin of
    Cain
Nothing remained of life on earth, it would now have a second
    birth
So Noah and his children, three, started all life a people free
For God had formed a brand new plan a new beginning for man
Thus through the sons of Noah earth's life began again
And yet ere long the die was cast, Nimrod was all too vain
This man had built a tower to reach the heaven that rained
He thought to fight against the God, the One through whom he
    pained
But soon he heard that God's Word could in no way be breached
Again there was a warning, God's outstretched arm had reached
All men were under judgment no longer speak the same
Yet out of this great scattering God's blessings fell like rain
For God raised up a heavenly hope for all men still in pain
Through Abram was the promise, God's man He soon would
    reign

**"And I will bless them that bless thee, and curse him that
curseth thee: and in thee shall all the families of the earth be
blessed" (Gen.12:3)**

## 18. WITHIN GOD'S REACH

So when the man had fallen God put in place a plan
To guide men's feet God saw it meet to be the Son of Man
So blood was shed and sin now fled
A way to raise man from the dead

The firstborn child was Cain for Eve had given birth
In every sense a rebel, a scourge upon the earth
Dishonored he his father rejected God's full plan
Not caring that his mother, thought him the Son of Man

A vagabond Cain had become, and head of a new breed
Who turned away from righteousness to self to meet his need
Descendants of this Cain were carnal too, each one
Lamech he married two wives and murdered men for fun

Thus ends the song of Cain who thought God's method vain
Following in the footsteps, of him God made to reign
His father failed The Father, and ate what should not be
His son in turn had on his own rebelled for all to see

Fruits of the fall were sinners like Cain
But no man's life need be in vain
For you and for me God has a great plan
The Bible it tells us, "Salvation for man"

And if by some chance you don't find God's place
Remember that He has reached out by His grace
The windows of heaven are open to you
God is within reach what'err we may do

**"And the Word was made flesh and dwelt among us...
full of grace and truth" (John 1:14)**

## 19. NO SCARS NO DEATH

So often man's oppressions are burdens of the flesh
But few shrink back, or cry alarm
When soul and mind are done much harm
And all of life's enmeshed

The scars inflicted on the flesh
May leave some marks that heal
But havoc wrought upon the mind
Leaves traces that are hard to find, we kneel

The sons of God were heaven bound
They sought the Promised Land
But Pharaoh kept them to the task
Deliverer must be found

They'd served for some four hundred years
Deprived, impounded, brought to tears
Until the man of God arose
Threatening Pharaoh and all that opposed

This very Moses, He's the man
Who engineered God's Divine plan
Through plagues and Passover and plan,
Freedom at last, the Red Sea dry land

The furnace of Egypt left scars for all to see
The agony of slavery held back the victory
But by Passover God's angels set them free
So now at last Egypt was past, onwards to liberty

They journeyed to the Promised Land
With Joshua and God's Holy band
And soon they lived on, without fear
Their God Jehovah ever near

The days of bonds and agony
Of Joseph and Pharaoh and children yet to be
Were integrated in God's plan
Fulfilled at last in the Promised Land

The slave was dead but in his place
Arose the promise of a new race
Elijah, King David, had stirred the pot
And ultimately the Son of God was not

But in His sojourn here on earth
He gave new life by second birth
The scars that laid upon His back
Could'nt hinder the soul in its heavenly track

So too then turn away from death
The Shepherd is calling you'll never regret
No fuss, no fret, repent, have life
For you no death, no pain, no whip, no strife

The havoc wrought upon the sinful mind
Leaves echoes mirrored in the Cross Divine
The Savior's Blood removed all stain
The people of God did not "slave" in vain

**"...with His stripes We are healed"
(Isaiah 53:5)**

## 20. GOD'S MASTER PLAN (Gen.2:2, 3)

God had said it and t'was so, He had created Light
He used it to 'dispel', not put the dark to flight
For God had made the darkness rebellion to control
A place for fallen angels who spurned their heavenly role

And then God brought together the darkness and the light
Bound up in one equation He called them day and night
Thus in this way time came to mark
The judgment day for all that's Dark

When God formed the material world he said "Let there be
Light"
Limiting the range and scope of angels who would fight
Then brought together Judgment Day 'twas unified with death
And everything material was subject to that "threat"

To crown it all God then made man
The centerpiece of His Divine plan
To him our God then gave control
To choose obedience or lose his soul

He gave the man the power to face
To conquer darkness or threaten the race
God made a safehouse, He called it Eden
Man in control of all God's garden

But even in Eden's material life
An entry was made for darkness and strife
For in man's hand God placed His plan
To control darkness on the land

So into the life of the man there now came
A woman Divine Eve was her name
The tempter moved in, a serpent was he
Debated and argued of God's special the special tree

Before long the woman came under control
Tossed the Divine key, the obedience it holds
A victim she fell to the wiles of the snake
Adam also tempted, caught by her mistake

So thus through the serpent "dark" had control
And Satan gained power of all God's new world
But God had in place a deep master plan
To wrestle with Satan and win back the man

"Sabbath to the rescue," God's sanctified day
A place in creation where time had no sway
Divine common ground that blended in one
God's life all Eternal a day never done

**"And God blessed the seventh day and sanctified it"**
**(Gen.2:3)**

# CHAPTER FIVE

# FICKLE FAITH

### 21. SAMARITAN OR STRANGER

So motionless alone he lay
A crumpled heap along the way
The hand of crime had found a mark
No help in sight but not yet dark

Footsteps are heard
Now drawing near
His hopes are high, Pastor is here
Surely, I know that he will care

"Not so, not so" this Pastor thought
He crossed the street
Stopping for naught
Just thanking God it was not he
Caught up in that catastrophe

But soon new footsteps, many more
Bibles in hand, Christians for sure
These folk are known, some seen of late
Giving out tracts before the gate
But they were busy, RAN from me
Saying aloud "May God's will be"

All hope seemed gone, faded away
The setting sun would end my day
Could be more woe, I hope not so
NEW STEPS I hear? That could not be
Did I hear someone calling ME

Again it came, the call, "who's there?"
The caller was lame, in a wheelchair
Messenger of hope indeed he was
And soon the place was all abuzz
I felt a gentle hand on me, somewhere behind I could not
see

The siren sounded, help was here
All was relief I had no fear
I asked the helper for his name
*"Doulos"* he said, for Christ, not fame
"Samaritan, that's why I came"

**"But a certain Samaritan as he journeyed, came where he was... and had compassion on him" (Luke 10:33)**

## 22. TOMORROW IS TODAY (Heb.4:7b)

Living is made up of snippets of time
When well-integrated life can be sublime
The "dos" and the "donts" that make up our day
Footprints to tomorrow are fashioned this way

So hasten to answer and do not delay
Examine your doings they'll show you the way
They flame you and fashion your life come what may
So careful my brother/sister tomorrow is today

The Lord He has told us to watch and to pray
This was not a reference to what others say
T'is just a reminder to us come what may
Tomorrow's temptation is fashioned today

So watch out my brother what you do'll hold sway
Though the Lord may forgive you for having your way
But history remembers it stores our todays
It serves to remind us of stumblings, bad ways

Each life it is made up of ups and of downs
Of times to be laughing and times that we frown
But often when frowning should come in our way
We cry "oh distress" tis too hard to say

For we are not made of finer stuff
To grin and to bear it eating dust
Our senses are an easy bruise
When pleasure is pain its hard to muse

What then the path that we must take
True constancy is hard to fake
Awake and live bad times will pass
No matter how dreadful the storm will not last

But bear this in mind a treasure you'll find
In all of life's issues whatever the kind
Yesterday's shadows will follow today
Yesterday was today when tomorrow was that way

There is a you beyond all pain
The Lord has come and not risen in vain
So cheer up my brother though storms are ahead
Our Jesus is Risen He's no longer dead

Lean hard on His way He'll see you through
Trust in His Word that's all you must do
He'll turn tomorrow's darkness into light today
Your loss would be gain God has the final say

**"Boast not thyself of to morrow; for thou knowest not
what a day may bring forth" (Proverbs 27:1)**

## 23. HOW NOW FOOL!

The Fool has said within his heart
"No God can ever be"
He finds it hard to look to Heaven
The Hand of God to See
And horrors "No" he must reject
The Word of God in Me
Since he's a fool and like a Mule
His stubborn stand will set the Rule
That says the creature's not a tool

But as it is, he's not content
To keep his thoughts within
He must make known all must be shown
The Wisdom given to him
So with his friends and with his foes
He shares his new-found knowledge
He is a learned man you know
He passed through the best College

And thus he speaks of earth and heaven
And how it came to be
It's "Mother Nature" not our God
Who formed the heavens and me
For as to man he just evolved
No dust has given him birth
The Stars, the Sun, the Moon, the heavens
Were formed just as the earth
All these have come to be in time
No God has set them so

That fool has blanketed his mind
He'll fight and struggle as will his kind
To move from real to the sublime
Without a thought that even his mind
Reflects a being of his kind
God's image is no pantomime

**"The fool hath said in his heart,
There is no God" (Psalm 53:1)**

## 24. TIME'S MISSION

Tomorrow lies beyond my reach
And yesterday is gone
Today is slipping fast by me
Evening was sometime morn

And as I ponder passing time
It soon is clear to me
That God has set in mot-ion
The lives of all who "be"

No standing still from birth until
The death-watch comes to call
Birthing itself is dying
Time path is meant for all

And as we think about it
It surely does seem true
That all our days under the sun
Are tuned to make us new

God gives the Grace time is the space
That God has put in motion
By hearing, turning to His word
New birth is life's own potion

So listen well go forth and tell
Each life must be a mission
To turn each "you" from death and hell
"Redeemed" the new condition

**"But know thou, that for all these things God will bring thee into Judgment" (Eccles.11:9)**

48

## 25. MY FRAME OF REFERENCE

At times I've often wondered
What frames a man, the me
Is it my thoughts, my fantasies
Of what I think should be
I hear the patter of their feet
As many folks pass by
Is it their destination
Does that determine "why"
So if by chance I know the "why"
The "what" and "where" may come
Do these together tell me
The place where I am from
But then there 're folks who never
Leave one place for another
They are forever sitting, liming
No worry, nothing seems to bother
What is their lot, all nature?
Has nurture been in vain
Are idle hands all destined
To live a life of pain?
But then its time to reckon
That life is so much more
No simple plan or gesture
Will measure all before
For God is in the picture
There's much more at my door
Man is His prime creation
To man there's so-o-o-o much more
The body's not the whole, like bird, or pig, or mole
The mind is really where, life shapes me, here or there
These, only God can see, they are the frame of me

**"Remember now thy Creator in the days of thy youth,
while the evil days come not" (Eccles.12:1)**

49

## 26. DIVINE JUSTICE

We think of Laws that Rule the land
And Governments that make them
We think of "Regs." that guide the hand
Of men who try to break them

There must be other laws as well
The tides, the heavens and where men dwell
Are bound by these, some men can't tell
The difference `tween a Heaven and a Hell

The Bible tells us of a Law
By which Death's Power is at the door
Of every man and every child
From Adam and Moses the good and the Vile

Yet all these Laws that Rule and Guide
The Heavens and Earth the men who Hide
May sometimes change, adjust or Bend
As terms, conditions reject, amend

But one Law Stands that Never Bends
Has scant regard for foes or friends
Inflexible it cannot change
God's Divine Justice has full range

God says that "whoso digs a pit
Shall fall in it" full pace to wit
Or if you chance to Roll a stone
To crush another, break his bone

Then know for sure the hand upraised
To strike at men and not to praise
Shall surely fall upon the head
Of him who strives to see them dead

This Law allows for no Appeal
No room to bend or wheel and deal
God's Divine Justice is at work
So, "humble Self" the Master spoke

**"Be not deceived; God is not mocked;**
**For whatsoever a man soweth, that shall he also reap"**
**(Gal.6:7)**

CHAPTER SIX

# ETERNAL LIFE FOR ALL?

### 27. WILL SURELY DIE

Dust thou art to dust return
Does not reflect the soul's sojourn
For when God said "Eat not that fruit"
He set in place the law of truth
Upon this law the soul is bound
Until obe**die**nce is found
And man has learned that every hour
From God to draw his strength and power
Man's soul is made of finer stuff
Than special clay or chosen dust
God from within His nature breathed
"Nephesh" emerged to be God's seed
The image of God that was the plan
Breathed out to form the soul of man
That in the ages yet to be
Man may yet spend eternity
The soul of man can surely die
But not to dust return
From God's fair presence it can fly
And in the lake will burn
All flesh in time may turn to dust
But souls of men forever must
Find rest in God, eternal trust
Or to the lake of fire will go
For all eternity that's so

**"Thou takest away their breath, they die, and return to their dust" (Ps.104:29)**
**"...not found written in the Book of Life was cast into the lake of fire" (Rev.20:15)**

## 28. TO DIE IS GAIN

Giving is getting
When God is in control
Sowing is reaping
When Christ has made you whole

Losing is finding
When grace has set you free
Dying is living
That's how it ought to be

But giving and sowing
Or losing and dying
Aren't what they seem to be
If Christ does not in you abide
From sin to set you free

So, press on now children
Reach out and feel God's touch
For at this very moment His hand is stretched out much
God waits to hear your faintest cry
His mercy lifts and burdens fly

What then dear, dear
Why linger here
Where fear and folly bring a tear
The God of Grace opens the door
For life with Him forever more

**"For me to live is Christ,
and to die is gain" (Phil.1:21)**

## 29. BY FAITH OR FANTASY?

The Word was preached and men were saved
All pledged to follow to the grave
But words and deeds don't often match
Some say "I'm saved" but there's a catch

A man named Achan in God's company
Lost faith on the journey by what he did see
For while in the battle he saw the *cursed* thing
Decided that these to his wife he will bring

For Achan had seen some things that he loved
He longed to receive them as gifts from above
So sneaking about to the city he went
He claimed the *accursed,* hid it in his tent

The journey continued the battle began
God's Spirit was leading, God wanted each man
But then upon all things God had put a curse
"The riches of Jericho were not for man's purse"

So through Achan's stumble Israel met defeat
God's people were humbled, something was not meet
The sin in the camp had stood in the way
God's army's in judgment when one disobey(s)

The Bible speaks much of some with "God talk"
Like Eli, or Judas, or Lot at Sodom's walk
But real faith lies not in man's words or his ways
God's power remakes what man's heart will crave

To envy or strive with thy brother today
Is not of God's wisdom *self* stands in the way
The wisdom of God that comes from above
Shows forth itself always, transcending our love

So please will you check on your heart-cry today
Is your faith just words or to obey what God say
If envy and malice still lie at your door
Make room to join Achan your judgment is sure

Take heed then my brother pray God its not true
That you are not planning for Heaven but Hell's view
Remember the scripture its not what we say
But life that surrenders will lead us God's way

**"And Joshua, and all Israel with him, took Achan...**
**And all Israel stoned him with stones,**
**and burned them with fire..." (Joshua.7:24, 25)**

## 30. WRONG ROAD

Tis Sunday I must go to Church
No fuss no delay, I'm quite in a lurch
Most of us here are glad to get there
The present life crises have caused us to fear

But Sunday is gone, ahhh life's back to normal
No Bible no praying all that's too formal
Our God up in heaven He sees in our heart
We don't have to tell Him, we're doing our part

And so goes the story the false way to glory
Yet many there be who live by this story
Content with the way that "seems right" they say
Though the sign at the end tells them "**hell is this way**"

Which road are you taking I hope you're not faking
This "wrong road" and "right road" is serious stuff
It won't do to feel you're on the right track
When hell is ahead all you do is turn back

"Faith only" the answer, it comes with God's Word
If you hear "the cock crowing" it's no mocking bird
For Peter it sounded the voice of alarm
The Word of the Savior had kept him from harm

In your case or mine there's no cock that's true
But Jesus has said His Voice only will do
So hear it, receive it, He knocks at our door
His Way leads to Glory, in Him, victory is sure

**"...That this night, before the cock crow,
Thou shalt deny me thrice" (Matthew 26:34)**

## 31. CHRISTMAS IN SODOM

While shepherds watched their flocks by night
The angels came to sing
And when they came to Sodom's gate
The same good news did bring

The shepherds learned that very night
That Jesus came to shed God's light
Lot, too, received the message clear
For him salvation very near

The messages were both the same
They spoke of deliverance, salvation to gain
The shepherds were told the Savior they'd meet
And God kept for Lot, in heaven, a seat

This very same news the angels will bring
To anyone seeking the Savior as King
Salvation for all, deliverance from death
And even in Sodom, the righteous are kept

All praise to our God, He saves us from Hell
His mercies extend to who in Him dwell
From sin he delivers all men who believe
He offers His Grace, did you yet receive?

**"And while he lingered, the men laid hold upon his hand
...the LORD being merciful unto him: and they brought him
forth, and set him without the city" (Genesis 19:16)**

## 32. JOY TO THE WORLD

My heart was full of joy
I clutched my Christmas toy
Just what I wanted all along
For all that day my life's, a song

But Christmas day had passed away
The toy I loved had lost its "say"
It stirred no more the joys in me
That feeling was pure fantasy

And so it seems today a toy
But by tomorrow some new joy
Must take the place of what seemed right
My days, my moments are in flight

All life it seems involves mere seconds
Glimpses of peace or joy that beckons
But once achieved have little meaning
My soul cries "more" to keep me beaming

But God has made it clear to me
My life is more than ecstasy
My time, my breath, I give to Him
He Only brings real peace within

So Christmas has passed a New Year is dawning
Your soul must find strength for each day, each morning
Turn away now from toy and empty pleasure
In Jesus you'll find real joy without measure

**"Love not the world,
neither the things that are in the world"
(1 John 2:15)**

# SUMMARY

The mind of man may journey to any destination, anywhere at anytime. But the journeys of the mind may not often be congruent with the will and purposes of God. The poems which are included in this publication are reflections of different journeys, at different times by people who may be far removed one from the other. But the conclusions in the Word of God apply equally to all men.

That God should reveal Himself to man is itself amazing. But that God should become man and put His Grace within the reach of all men is simply fantastic. Each poem in this collection was a vehicle for conveying some deep truth imbedded in God's Word. It is our hope that these verses make it easier for readers of every age to understand some basic Bible principles which sometimes may seem quite complex.

# ABOUT THE AUTHOR

Roderick Loney is the Pastor of Beth'aleel Fundamental Baptist Church in San Fernando, Trinidad and Tobago, where he maintains voluntary ministries to the larger community. He is a graduate of Moody Bible Institute and earned a B.A. in Bible Archaeology and M.A. in Church History from Wheaton College. At Columbia University he completed a Doctor of Education (Ed. D.) and a Ph.D. in Stress Management Psychology at Clayton University.

He is also the author of "The Inner Faces of Mercy."

www.ingramcontent.com/pod-product-compliance
Lightning Source LLC
Chambersburg PA
CBHW060717030426
42337CB00017B/2902